PORTRAITS OF THE STATES

★ ★

WASHINGTON

by P. M. Boekhoff and
Jonatha A. Brown

GARETH**STEVENS**
PUBLISHING
A Member of the WRC Media Family of Companies

Please visit our web site at: www.garethstevens.com
For a free color catalog describing Gareth Stevens Publishing's
list of high-quality books and multimedia programs, call
1-800-542-2595 (USA) or 1-800-387-3178 (Canada).
Gareth Stevens Publishing's fax: (414) 332-3567.

Library of Congress Cataloging-in-Publication Data

Boekhoff, P. M. (Patti Marlene), 1957-
    Washington / P. M. Boekhoff and Jonatha A. Brown.
      p. cm. — (Portraits of the states)
    Includes bibliographical references and index.
    ISBN 0-8368-4637-0 (lib. bdg.)
    ISBN 0-8368-4656-7 (softcover)
    1. Washington (State)—Juvenile literature. I. Brown, Jonatha A.
    II. Title. III. Series.
    F891.3.B43   2005
    979.7—dc22   2005042671

This edition first published in 2006 by
Gareth Stevens Publishing
A Member of the WRC Media Family of Companies
330 West Olive Street, Suite 100
Milwaukee, WI 53212 USA

This edition copyright © 2006 by Gareth Stevens, Inc.

Editorial direction: Mark J. Sachner
Project manager: Jonatha A. Brown
Editor: Betsy Rasmussen
Art direction and design: Tammy West
Picture research: Diane Laska-Swanke
Indexer: Walter Kronenberg
Production: Jessica Morris and Robert Kraus

Picture credits: Cover, p. 15 © CORBIS; pp. 4, 21, 22, 24, 25, 26, 28 © Gibson
Stock Photography; pp. 5, 9, 20 © Corel; p. 6 © PhotoDisc; p. 8 © Art Today;
p. 10 University of Washington Libraries, Special Collections, NA2217;
p. 11 © James P. Rowan; p. 16 University of Washington Libraries,
Special Collections, NA4117; p. 27 © Hulton Archive/Getty Images;
p. 29 © Otto Greule Jr./Getty Images

Printed in the United States of America

1 2 3 4 5 6 7 8 9 09 08 07 06 05

CONTENTS

Words that are defined in the Glossary appear
in **bold** the first time they are used in the text.

On the Cover: The Space Needle (far right) is the highlight of
Seattle's skyline.

Introduction

Would you like to see an active volcano? Would you like to fish for salmon, walk through a rain forest, or hike up a snow-covered mountain? You can do all those things and more in Washington.

Washington is an amazing state. It has mountains, rain forests, and grasslands. It has miles of ocean shoreline and one of the biggest rivers in the United States. It also has large cities, some of which are very beautiful. The state has a rich history, too.

Many people who live in Washington would never want to live anywhere else!

Snow-capped peaks and clear blue lakes make North Cascades National Park a very special place.

Potlatches

The Chinook and the Coast Salish held **ceremonies** called potlatches. People made speeches and had a feast. The person who held the potlatch gave gifts to every guest. The gifts showed how rich and important the giver was.

from the Rocky Mountains. Meriwether Lewis and William Clark led this group. They went back East full of praise for the rich land they had seen. Before long, many fur traders came.

One Land, Many Masters

Three countries now wanted to control the whole Northwest. They were Spain, Britain, and the United States. All three wanted to grow rich from the fur trade.

leading the way. He traded with the Natives and left with many otter furs. Other British explorers and traders followed. Britain and Spain agreed to share the rich area.

In the late 1700s, an American, Robert Gray, sailed along the coast and up the Columbia River. In 1805, an American team reached the area by canoeing down rivers that flowed

IN WASHINGTON'S HISTORY

A True Story or a Tall Tale?
In Italy in 1596, a Greek sailor claimed to have seen the area we call Washington. This sailor went by the name Juan de Fuca. He said he had sailed there on a Spanish ship in 1592. No one knew whether his story was true. Even so, the Juan de Fuca **Strait** was later named for him.

IN WASHINGTON'S HISTORY

Early Missionaries

Marcus Whitman and Henry Spalding came to Washington in 1836. They wanted to teach the Natives about God. They were **missionaries**. Their wives came, too. They were the first white women to live in the area. Years later, Natives attacked and killed them all. Even so, more missionaries followed.

Before long, however, Spain gave up its claims. Britain and the United States agreed to take turns. Each would control the land for ten years. This agreement worked for thirty years. In 1846, Britain and the United States split the area.

Famous People of Washington

Chief Joseph

Born: About 1840, Wallowa Valley, Oregon Territory

Died: September 21, 1904, Colville **Reservation**, Washington

Chief Joseph was a Nez Percé leader. In 1877, the U.S. government wanted the Nez Percé to move to a reservation in Idaho. Chief Joseph tried to lead his people to Canada instead. The U.S. Army chased them, and the Natives held them off for months. Many people came to respect Chief Joseph. He treated prisoners well. He took care of women and children, too. The army finally caught them. Chief Joseph and his people were sent to a reservation far away. It was a sad ending to their struggle for freedom.

Now Washington belonged to the United States.

Washington Territory

Washington **Territory** was formed in 1853. Isaac Stevens was its first governor. His job was to get land from the Natives. He asked the to sign **treaties** in which they agreed to leave their land. Many tribes did not understand these treaties. They did not realize that they were unfair. Many Native groups signed the treaties.

IN WASHINGTON'S HISTORY

The Oregon Trail
In the 1800s, thousands of people moved to Washington. Most came in horse-drawn wagons by way of the Oregon Trail. This trail was 2,000 miles (3,200 km) long. It stretched from Missouri to Washington. The trip took from four to six months and was a long, hard journey.

Horses pulled wagons like these along the Oregon Trail. It was a long, dusty trip.

9

This Nez Percé family posed for pictures in 1909.

reached the area for the first time. Now that settlers could ride on trains, they came to Washington by the thousands.

Now, white people owned the land, yet the Natives had not meant for this to happen. They fought to get their land back. From 1855 to 1858, they fought the settlers and the U.S. Army. Finally, the army beat them. The Natives were forced to move to reservations, and settlers took over the land.

For a long time, travel to Washington was very difficult. It became easier in 1883. That year, a railroad

Some settlers became sheep ranchers. Others planted wheat, fruits, and vegetables. Many worked on the railroads or in the forests, where they cut down trees for lumber. Some worked in mines.

Growing Pains

In 1889, Washington became a U.S. state. More and more people moved to the area. Some of the new arrivals

FUN FACTS

The World's Fair

The World's Fair was held in Seattle in 1962. The city leaders rebuilt much of Seattle for this event. They wanted to show the world of the future. To get this idea across, they built a tall skinny building. They called it the Space Needle. It reached high into the sky and did not look like other buildings. The fair and the Space Needle drew millions of people to Seattle. Even now, people still visit the city to see the Space Needle.

People can go up to the observation deck on the Space Needle. It is 520 feet (159 m) above the ground.

came from China. White people did not always welcome them. They were afraid the Chinese would take jobs away from them.

In the early 1940s, World War II raged. Many men left Washington to fight. Yet farmers there still needed people to harvest their crops. They brought workers to the state from Mexico and other Latin

Every Vote Counts!
In November 2004, more than 2.7 million people cast votes in the governor's race. The results were so close that the votes had to be counted three times. Christine Gregoire won by 130 votes.

countries. After the war, people continued to settle there. Some were Asians or African Americans.

The state grew quickly, but it continued to have problems. One problem was that many waterways became **polluted**. Lake Washington was one of the worst. People in the state took the problems seriously. They cleaned up the water. Now they take care of the lakes, rivers, and forests.

Another problem involved fishing. By the early 1970s, fewer and fewer fish were found in the rivers. Big fishing companies had caught too many fish. Natives caught fish, too. Some people thought the Natives should stop fishing. The Natives disagreed. A treaty signed in the 1850s gave them the right to fish. In 1974, the **issue** went to court. The judge said the treaty could not be broken. The Natives could keep fishing. The Natives and other people who cared about the fish had to learn to work together to protect them.

In November 1999, the World Trade Organization (WTO) met in Seattle. Many felt that the work the WTO was doing hurt poor nations. Thousands turned out in the streets to **protest**.

1775	Spanish explorers claim Washington for Spain.
1805	Lewis and Clark reach the Pacific Ocean by following rivers.
1853	Washington Territory is set up.
1855–1858	Native Americans fight to keep their land.
1877	Chief Joseph tries to flee to Canada with many Nez Percé, but they are caught and sent to a reservation.
1883	A railroad first connects Washington to other parts of the country.
1889	Washington becomes the 42nd U.S. state.
1942	Japanese Americans are taken from Washington and forced to live in camps.
1962	The World's Fair is held in Seattle.
1974	Judge says treaty with Natives can't be broken.
1980	Mt. St. Helens **erupts**.
1991	Spilled oil from a ship covers the shore of Olympic National Park.
1999	World Trade Organization (WTO) meets in Seattle and is protested by some.
2004-2005	Christine Gregoire wins the governor's race by only a few votes.

People

Mᵒre than six million people live in Washington. Most live in or near cities in the western part of the state. In fact, more than half of the people in Washington live in or around the cities of Seattle and Tacoma. The eastern half of the state has fewer people. Most of them live in or near the city of Spokane.

Early Growth

Many Chinese came to the state in the late 1800s and early 1900s. They worked on

Hispanics: In the 2000 U.S. Census, 7.5 percent of the people in Washington called themselves Latino or Hispanic. Most of them or their relatives came from places where Spanish is spoken. They may come from different racial back-grounds.

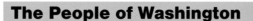
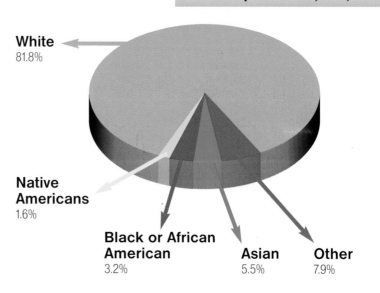

The People of Washington

Total Population 6,203,788

White 81.8%

Native Americans 1.6%

Black or African American 3.2%

Asian 5.5%

Other 7.9%

Percentages are based on the 2000 Census.

14

Seattle is the largest city in Washington. Almost 600,000 people live there.

the railroads and in coal mines. African Americans from the East moved to Washington, too. They came to work in the mines. Europeans also flocked to Washington. Most came from Britain, Italy, Russia, and Sweden. They found jobs in **factories** and on farms. By 1910, half of the people in the state had been born in another country.

During this time, people poured into the state from Japan, too. They had heard that the United States was a good place to find jobs.

A Serious Mistake

The United States entered World War II in 1941. It fought against Japan and other countries. By this time, thousands of Japanese Americans lived in Washington. Their presence there worried some people, who were afraid the Japanese Americans might be **spies**.

They thought they might be trying to help Japan.

Before long, the U.S. government made all Japanese Americans leave the coast of the Northwest. These people had done nothing wrong, yet they had to move inland. They were forced to live in crowded camps for the rest of the war. Most of them lost everything they owned.

Years later, the U.S. government said it was sorry for sending the Japanese away. It gave money to the Japanese Americans who had lived in the camps. By then, most of the **victims** had died or moved far away.

In the early 1900s, these boys were on the baseball team at the Spokane Indian School.

The People Today

All kinds of people live in Washington today. About eight people in one hundred are Hispanic. Fewer are Asian or Native American. Even so, more Asians and Natives live in this state than most other U.S. states.

In 1996, Washington made U.S. history. That year, Gary Locke became governor. He was the first Chinese American ever elected to this post.

Education and Religion

The first two schools in Washington opened in the 1830s. One was for Native children, and the other was for white children. About thirty years later, the University of Washington opened. Today, it has schools in three cities. The state has many other universities and colleges, too.

Three out of four people in Washington are Christians. Most of these Christians are Protestants. Fewer are Catholic. The state is also home to Jews, Buddhists, and people of other religions.

Famous People of Washington

Frank Herbert

Born: October 8, 1920, Tacoma, Washington

Died: Died: February 11, 1986, Madison, Wisconsin

Frank Herbert was a science fiction writer. He wrote about what life might be like in other worlds. One of his early books was *Dune*. He showed this story to twenty publishers, and every one turned it down. Herbert finally found a publisher in 1965. *Dune* was an immediate hit! After that, Herbert wrote five more books based on the same idea. His books are still popular today.

The Land

Washington is known as "The Evergreen State" because about half of its land is covered with lush, green forests. Yet Washington is not green all over. Parts of the state are very dry. In some places, the landscape is often more brown than green.

The East

The eastern part of the state is fairly dry. It gets little rain or snow. It is hot in the summer and cold in the winter.

Much of the land is low, rolling hills. Farms cover huge areas. Where the land is still wild, grasses and sagebrush grow.

The Cascades

To the west of the grasslands are the Cascade Mountains. The western slopes of the mountains get lots of rain and snow, while the eastern slopes get very little. Many different animals can be found in the

WASHINGTON

CANADA

Ross L.
Ross Lake NRA
Okanogan R.
Columbia R.
Pend Oreille R.

San Juan Islands

Bellingham

Juan de Fuca Strait

North Cascades NP

Lake Chelan NRA
L. Chelan

Franklin D. Roosevelt L.

Olympic Mountains

Puget Sound
Everett
Seattle
Bellevue

Cascade Range

Spokane R.
Banks L.
Grand Coulee Dam NRA
Spokane

Olympic NP

Tacoma
Lakes District
Mt. Rainier NP

Wenatchee Mountains

Columbia Basin

IDAHO

Harbor

Olympia

Pacific Ocean

Mt. Rainier

Yakima
Mt. Adams

Snake R.

L. Sacajawea

L. Wallula

Longview
Mt. St. Helens

L. Umatilla

Vancouver

Columbia R.

OREGON

SCALE/KEY

0   100 Miles

0   100 Kilometers

⭐ State Capital

🔺 Highest Point

Mountains

N
W   E
S

mountains. Mountain lions, mountain goats, and even grizzly bears make their homes there.

Volcanoes formed the Cascades long ago. Most of these volcanoes are **extinct**, but a few are still active. Mt. Rainier is an active volcano. At 14,410 feet (4,392 meters) above sea level, it is the highest point in the state.

Mt. St. Helens erupted in 1980. The explosion took

1,300 feet (396 m) off the top of the mountain! Ash and rocks flew through the air, and huge trees became piles of sticks. Since then, the plants and trees have started growing back.

The Coast

The land around Puget Sound tends to be low. The land between the sound and the ocean is more mountainous.

The Olympic Mountains rise up from a big rain forest. Most of the trees in the rain forest are pine and other evergreens. Douglas Firs are the tallest trees in the state. Herds of elk live in this area. Deer and black bear live here, too. Killer whales swim off the coast.

Major Rivers
Columbia River
1,214 miles (1,953 km) long
Snake River
1,038 miles (1,670 km) long
Spokane River
120 miles (195 km) long

Mt. St. Helens is still an active volcano. Scientists keep a close eye on it. They want to let people know if it is going to erupt.

Many parts of Washington are still wilderness. These tree-covered mountains are in Olympic National Park.

River. Like other rivers in the state, it flows into the Pacific Ocean. A huge dam has been built across this river. It slows the flow of water, so a big lake forms behind it. This dam, the Grand Coulee, is the biggest dam in the country.

This part of the state receives a great deal of rain. The weather is usually mild, but snow falls in the mountains.

Earthquakes sometimes shake the area around Puget Sound. In February 2001, a strong quake was felt near Olympia. Buildings were damaged. Hundreds of people were hurt, but no one was killed.

Columbia River

Washington has many rivers. The largest is the Columbia

FUN FACTS

Salmon

Five kinds of salmon live in Washington. These fish are as interesting as they are beautiful. They are born in freshwater rivers and, while they are babies, they swim downstream to the sea. They live in the ocean until they are fully grown. Finally, they swim back up the river to where they were born and lay eggs. Their babies hatch in freshwater and start the **cycle** again.

CHAPTER 5

Economy

Washington is a big producer of electrical power. In fact, it provides one-third of all water-based electricity in the country! This power comes from dams on rivers. The state has more than one thousand dams.

Many of the state's rivers also provide fish. Some fish are caught in the wild, while others are grown on fish farms.

Forests and Farming

Washington has more forests than any other U.S. state. The forests supply wood to logging companies and homes to wildlife. The state works hard to keep its forests healthy.

The Boeing plant in Everett is huge. It takes a lot of space to build airplanes!

22

Washington is the number one producer of apples, dried peas, and pears in the nation. Even so, wheat is its biggest farm crop. Other vegetables, fruits, and hay are grown in Washington, too. Dairy and chicken farms dot the land near Puget Sound.

Other Businesses

Many companies are located in Washington. Microsoft Corporation is based in Redmond. It makes computer **software**. The Boeing Company makes airplanes in Everett. Its factory there is the biggest building in the world.

Tourism also provides jobs. Tourists often eat at restaurants, stay at hotels, and visit parks. All of these places hire workers.

The state also has three major seaports — Seattle, Tacoma, and Grays Harbor.

How Money Is Made in Washington

Services* 25.0%

Mining 0.2%

Farming 2.1%

Building 4.9%

Buying and Selling to Businesses 6.9%

Transportation and Utilities (water, electricity, telephones) 7.9%

Buying and Selling to Consumers 9.8%

Making Goods 12.6%

Government 13.2%

Banking, Insurance, Property Sales 17.4%

* Services include jobs in hotels, restaurants, auto repair, medicine, teaching, and entertainment.

Government

Olympia is the capital of Washington. The state's leaders work there. The government has three parts, or branches. They are the executive, legislative, and judicial branches of government.

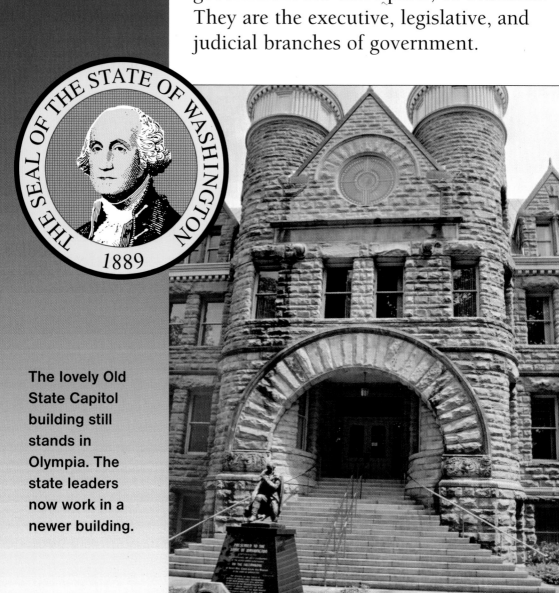

The lovely Old State Capitol building still stands in Olympia. The state leaders now work in a newer building.

The state legislature meets in this huge hall. The hall is part of the current state capitol building.

Executive Branch

The executive branch carries out the laws of the state. The governor is the leader of this branch. The lieutenant governor helps him or her.

Legislative Branch

The legislative branch is made up of the Senate and the House of Representatives. These two groups work together to make state laws.

Judicial Branch

This branch is made up of judges and courts. They often decide whether people who have been **accused of** committing crimes are guilty.

Local Governments

Washington has 39 counties and 280 cities or towns. Each city and county has its own leaders.

WASHINGTON'S STATE GOVERNMENT

Executive		Legislative		Judicial	
Office	**Length of Term**	**Body**	**Length of Term**	**Court**	**Length of Term**
Governor	4 years	Senate (49 members)	4 years	Supreme (9 justices)	6 years
Lieutenant Governor	4 years	House of Representatives (98 members)	2 years	Appeals (22 judges)	6 years

Things to See and Do

Many people who come to Washington visit Seattle first. They view totem poles and other art created by local Natives. The city has more than twenty art and history museums. The Experience Music Project is one of them. It focuses on the history of rock and roll.

Seattle has long had a hot music scene. Its symphony orchestra and opera companies are well known.

FUN FACTS

Underground City

Seattle was founded in 1851. It was built on low-lying land, so the streets were often wet and muddy. In 1889, a huge fire destroyed most of the city. A new city was built several feet above the old one. Some of the old roads and buildings were left below. Today, visitors go under the new city to see parts of the old one.

Burke Museum displays totems and other art made by Native Americans.

Jimi Hendrix

Born: November 27, 1942, Seattle, Washington

Died: September 18, 1970, London, England

Jimi Hendrix was born John Allen Hendrix. He was a great rock star. He sang and played guitar. Hendrix combined rock, jazz, blues, and soul music to create a new sound. He played the electric guitar in new ways, too. Some say he was the best rock guitarist who ever lived.

The city is also known for a kind of music called "grunge." Grunge was created in the 1980s. It is a blend of punk and heavy metal music. Seattle bands such as Nirvana and Pearl Jam became famous. These grunge bands changed the course of popular music.

Jimi Hendrix was an amazing guitar player. His style of playing changed rock music in the late 1960s.

Parks

Washington has three national parks. It also has more than 125 state parks. Park visitors hike through **ancient** forests. They climb peaks, go windsurfing, and fly kites.

Famous People of Washington

Bill Gates

Born: October 28, 1955, Seattle, Washington

Bill Gates has liked computers since he was a child. When he was a young man, he started a software company with his friend Paul Allen. They named the company Microsoft. The company is now based in Redmond. It makes all kinds of software. It makes everything from games to the operating systems that run computers. Bill Gates has become the richest man in the world. He and his wife, Melinda, use some of their money to help others. They try to help children all over the world stay healthy.

Hell's Canyon is on the Snake River. It is the deepest canyon in the country. Visitors admire the canyon as they float down the river on rafts.

Hell's Canyon delights both hikers and rafters.

Sports

Seattle has many big league sports teams. Fans flock to see the Seattle Mariners play baseball. The NBA (men's basketball) team is the SuperSonics. The WNBA (women's basketball) team is the Storm. The Seahawks are a popular football team.

A favorite winter sport is skiing. The Okanogan Highlands and the Cascades are great places to ski. Water sports are popular on Puget Sound.

Fairs and Festivals

Cities and towns around the state host all kinds of special events. Yakima is home to the state fair. Tacoma has a daffodil festival. Long Beach hosts an international kite festival. Seattle, Longview, and Bellingham are just a few of the places that hold music and dance festivals. The people of this state love to have a party!

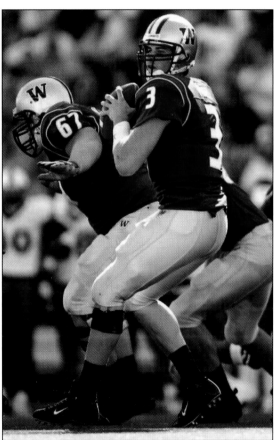

The Huskies play for the University of Washington. Thousands of football fans turn out for their games.

accused of — blamed for

ancient — very, very old

ceremonies — formal gatherings where activities follow a set pattern or plan

cycle — a pattern that starts and ends in the same place, like a circle

erupts — breaks out or explodes with great force

extinct — dead, inactive

factories — buildings where goods and products are made

issue — problem

missionaries — people who spread a religion

polluted — poisoned

protest — speak out against something

reservation — land held aside by the government for a particular use

software — electronic instructions that tell computers what to do

spies — people who watch others and report their secrets to an enemy

strait — a long, narrow body of water that connects one big body of water to another

territory — an area that belongs to a country

tourism — traveling for pleasure

treaties — written agreements

victims — people who have been wronged

Books

Brother Eagle, Sister Sky: A Message from Chief Seattle. Chief Seattle and Susan Jeffers (Scholastic Inc.)

Mount Saint Helens: The Smoking Mountain. Volcanoes of the World (series). Kathy Furgang (PowerKids Press)

A North American Rain Forest Scrapbook. Virginia Wright-Frierson (Walker and Co.)

People of Salmon and Cedar. Ron Hirschi (Cobblehill Books)

Washington Facts and Symbols. States and Their Symbols (series). Emily McAuliffe (Hilltop Books)

Web Sites

Burke Museum of Natural History and Culture
www.washington.edu/burkemuseum

Northwest Washington Kids' Page
www.plaidnet.com/kids

Washington State History Museum
www.wshs.org

Washington State Legislature Kid's Page
www.leg.wa.gov/common/kids

INDEX